CONTENTS

Foreword	v
Introduction	vii
Step #1 – Make a Commitment	13
Step #2 – Embrace the Reality	19
Step #3 – Allow the Recovery Process	29
Step #4 – Let Go	35
Step #5 – Create New Normals	39
Step #6 – Assess Yourself	45
Step #7 – Start Over	49
Step #8 – Embrace Your New	55
About the Author	61

STARTING OVER
*Tips For Recovery
After Personal Loss*

BRENDA DANIEL

Largo, MD

Copyright © 2017 Brenda Daniel

All rights reserved under the international copyright law. No part of this book may be reproduced or transmitted in any form or by any means, electronic or mechanical, including photocopying, recording, or by any information storage or retrieval system, without express written permission of the author or publisher. The exception is reviewers, who may quote brief passages for review.

Christian Living Books
P. O. Box 7584
Largo, MD 20792
christianlivingbooks.com
We bring your dreams to fruition.

ISBN Paperback 9781562293482
ISBN Electronic Version 9781562293499

Scripture quotations are taken from the New King James Version®. Copyright © 1982 by Thomas Nelson. Used by permission. All rights reserved.

Cover Illustration by Marco Bernard

Printed in the United States of America

INTRODUCTION

THE FOUR SCENARIOS I am about to share with you represent grave realities that no one is ever *really* prepared to face. Losing something or someone is never a pleasant experience. When the loss is something you are spiritually, emotionally, or physically connected to, it will always result in a time of crisis. These few are only a speck in the scope of the many adversities people face in life, but I use them as examples relative to my own personal experience with loss and recovery.

The first type of loss is *divorce.* A scenario would be something like this: A husband who brings news to his wife of 27 years that his answer for how to resolve an impasse in the marriage is that they separate which would then lead to divorce. So, we see here the death of a marriage or relationship.

The second is the loss of health. An individual goes for a routine checkup. After the doctor runs a series of tests, he comes back to the patient with the results, stating that he is about 90% sure he had discovered a cancerous mass.

What about the loss of a business or job? An employer summons the employee to their office only to regretfully inform them that "unfortunately today is your last day with the company."

Can you or perhaps someone you know relate to any of these scenarios yet? Let's consider one more. A family member answers the phone one day, only to hear from the other end that a terrible accident took place and a drunk driver hit their loved one, but by the time they reach them, they have died. Physical death is the most final kind of loss.

> *"Therefore know that the LORD YOUR GOD, HE is God, the faithful God who keeps covenant and mercy for a thousand generations with those who love Him and keep His commandments."* (Deuteronomy 7:9)

The pain and suffering that comes from either of these types of scenarios is devastating and instantly life altering, to say the least. In fact, depending on the nature of what you've lost and its significance to your life, recovery can seem to be far out of your reach. It's not an easy thing to handle when you realize that what you thought was the best of your life is taken away and no longer a part of the rest of your life.

My motivation for writing this book is that I am one of the billions of people who can relate to the life crisis of loss; more specifically, the kind of loss that changes your life, your world, and how you see and navigate through your world forever!

My desire is that you will find hope and strength as I share my testimony of personal loss; and what worked for me to get to the place of full recovery. I am fully persuaded that there are some who will read or hear this information and apply the principles to their own circumstances. They too will regain the courage to live a fulfilling life of new normals. I sure hope you are one of those people!

Now, having journeyed through to the other side of one of the most severe seasons of adversity and loss, I can say with great boldness and conviction… Life does not have to end in the overwhelming circumstances of what you've lost. But remember this: it will if you allow yourself to get stuck in the disparity of your loss and pain. The disparities I speak of are more specifically known as: sorrow, anger, fear, self-pity, guilt, unforgiveness, denial, pride, impatience, failure, and the likes. All these can potentially work together in your thinking to justify why you "will not" "cannot" and "should not" move forward to a healthy productive life.

So, this is how it went for me...

We've all heard of the old saying, "When it rains it pours." Well, unfortunately for me, in just a short, intense period of 18 months, I found myself faced with the reality of three of the worst life storms I had ever encountered. Back-to-back, this outpouring of loss –like the force of a tornado – literally shattered my life as I knew it. My life – the good or the bad of that life – it is what I lived and had become a part of for almost 30 years.

My husband of 27 years left me. Three months later after three attempts to get him to reconsider his decision, I filed divorce papers. I was broadsided with his decision, and the actual divorce was nothing less than death. With my head still spinning and my heart splattered over the ground, six months after papers were filed, a routine check-up revealed that I needed to have surgery immediately to remove a cancerous tumor if I wanted to live another six months! That blow felt as if the bottom was completely ripped out of my life. I had the major surgery, and a significant part of my colon was removed to ensure that clean margins were reached. Approximately nine months after surgery, while still emotionally broken, and in a physically fragile state, I was called into an office at work and told that the company I was employed with for 22 years was downsizing and my position was being phased out. I was let go!

Yes. I was now unemployed at 55, having to learn and re-learn an employment market that was extremely competitive, even for a much younger and current college graduate. Because my long-term work history was within a non-profit organization, there was no option for unemployment insurance. I was left with no means of supporting myself.

It was as though I had gotten caught up in a very strategic whirlwind with the intelligence to dismantle everything I knew as a way of life. The days, the weeks, and months to follow would be some of the most difficult I had ever encountered. In order to follow up on the cancer diagnosis, I had to resort to county clinics and hospitals. I could not afford a lease payment for housing, so I had to move in with friends. Everything was shut down for me and it was a very dark time.

What was meant to destroy me – and many days it felt like hopelessly destructive – actually turned out to be the place where I experienced God's power of love as never before. Now, having come through victoriously, it has proven to be one of the most defining and valuable seasons of my life to date.

This book, *Starting Over*, is not about all the gory details of everything that happened to me. Rather, it is about what it took for a 50+ year-old-woman to recover, be restored, and pull myself up from under Ground Zero. For me, it really was like the devastation of the World Trade Center on September 11, 2001. I am sharing things I did, was tempted to do, and what I didn't do. I knew the dangers of getting stuck, and I was determined with the help of God, to regain the courage to start my life over again. Equally important, I knew there was no easy or quick fix.

You will find, in this short read, seven practical must-do things that kept me from getting stuck in life after the devastation of personal loss and crisis. If you found the title of this book attractive enough to listen to or read, I can safely assume you may have experienced loss of a relationship, loss of an inheritance, loss of a job or business, loss of self-confidence, loss of a dream, loss of a life, or the loss of health. Everyone on the planet at one time or another will encounter one or more of these.

I want to encourage you with some good news… As hopeless and painful as your loss may have been, if at the end of it you are still breathing, you *can* recover; you *can* start over again, beginning today! I believe that if you have gotten this far in this book you are ready for change. When we are *really ready* for change, we find change! Now, let's get into the heart of the matter!

STEP 1

MAKE A COMMITMENT

YOUR FIRST STEP to accomplishing anything can be a bit intimidating. An even greater challenge is when we are faced with making a commitment to something, while still in a state of pain or disappointment caused by a previous commitment. The thought of opening yourself up again to the possibility of disappointment or pain is hard to ignore. In the case of personal loss, a firm commitment to the recovery process is the most difficult step. Commitment to recovery is summed up in three resolves:

1. I will not get stuck in this emotional storm.
2. My life does not end here.
3. I will recover.

I've learned that the longer you delay in making a decision for this to your goal, the longer it takes for the process of recovery. Anyone who has successfully gone through a great crisis of loss has at some point had these three resolves.

The question to ask yourself is this: "Do I stay in the reality of what used to be, or do I face where I am now and work to make what is left of my life worth living?" I submit to you that in order to have a bright future, you'll have to let one of the two realities go. Nothing good comes from trying to live life in your now while you are stuck and obsessing over what is no more.

Getting over what caused you so much pain may take you more time than others, but just keep in mind that it is doable. We all process life differently but your "commitment to recovery" coupled with God's grace on your life as a believer, will keep you moving forward in the midst of vulnerable and unsure feelings. I can remember when I was in recovery mode. Sometimes, I would grow impatient and tried to figure things out using my own reasoning. It would always end up in frustration and setbacks. I learned that impatience in the recovery process always led me to fearful actions. It would be such an emotional roller coaster because fear would always leave me feeling bleak about my future and discouraged.

Let God help you with your commitment. I or others can encourage you in this, but only you can convince yourself that your life is still worth living, and that true recovery is only found in Him. Fear is designed to control you. If you are the kind of person who spends your whole life trying to control everything, you are setting yourself up to be controlled by fear. Fulfillment in life does not come from trying to control it, but rather it comes when we live it in such a way that our choices and decisions will sustain us in the face of all the complexities of life and even death.

> Do I stay in the reality of what used to be, or do I face where I am now and work to make what is left of my life worth living?

"For God has not given us a spirit of fear, but of power and of love and of a sound mind." (2 Timothy 1:7)

Recovery begins with your thoughts. Leaving your thoughts unchecked eventually causes those fear-controlled thoughts to control your behavior. People who are driven and tormented by fear have no peace. When we experience the death of something or someone dear to us, it is in that vulnerable state of feeling out of control that we are more prone to allow fear to enter in.

The process to recover from a fear-driven life is to first make a decision that you will move forward.

Ironically enough, the answer for how to move forward is only realized after that decision is made. Although you may prefer to be left alone, and may not have the energy or the courage to do anything, what is most important at this stage is that a resolve is made in your mind and your heart that at some point you will do what it takes to begin to move forward. This decision will prove to be crucial in bringing a peaceful balance to your new life.

Have you ever noticed how it's so easy to become comfortable in fearful thoughts and behaviors? As tormenting as fear is, and even though it produces nothing good for your life, somehow we tend to have great tolerance for it. But to get past the many facades of fear, we literally have to *make* ourselves do what we know is good for us. It's not different than when parents *make* their children do those things which are necessary for them to grow up healthy, physically and emotionally. You made them eat veggies, you made them brush their teeth, you made them obey your instructions – and many times with great resistance. But, you made them do it anyway because it was the right thing to do.

I realize that because we are all so different in our make up and in the way we process life's adversities, there's no cookie-cutter formula for how to rebuild our lives after the altering trauma of loss. In fact, our circumstances are as unique as we are individually.

On the other hand, some principles are built into life and are universal in the results they produce. My personal experience with loss and recovery has taught me that the first step of committing to the recovery process is one of those. Do not let fear stop you from committing to your healthy future!

STEP 2

EMBRACE THE REALITY

WHEN YOU HAVE been broadsided with an unexpected loss, the blow can leave you in a dumbfounded state. Everything feels like a dream, like it didn't just happen to you. It's as if the mind shifts to a higher gear in order to do everything it can to protect the heart and separate it from the devastating pain or shock.

When that doctor walked into that recovery room and ever so casually announced that he found cancer in my body, and that I'd have to move quickly or I wouldn't live another six months, it was surreal! I actually told him, "You must have the wrong file. *My* name was Brenda Daniel!" I just figured it had to be a mistake because it was too serious for anyone to be so cavalier. It felt like this invisible wall of numbness rose up to hide the reality. Someone said this to me once, and I have learned that it really is true: "You cannot fix a problem that you do not have." Don't get me wrong, I never owned cancer as mine, but I certainly had to acknowledge that it manifested itself in my body. To ignore that and pretend it didn't exist would have been crazy. It would have simply meant that I was trying to escape the situation through denial and that is not the answer. As a matter of fact, that kind of thinking will only delay or prevent the process to recovery.

Think about your last dentist appointment. Remember what it felt like when the dentist gave you a shot to numb the area he was about to work on? Now think about how not only your mouth but your whole head felt when the anesthesia wore off. The pain from the drilling, cutting, swelling, or even the injection and extraction is felt with greater intensity.

It's a very subtle thing, but it is amazing how many defense mechanisms we come up with trying to anesthetize the pain after we have been hit hard by life—particularly personal losses.

"For I know the thoughts that I think toward you, says the LORD, thoughts of peace and not of evil, to give you a future and a hope." (Jeremiah 29:11)

Working hand in hand with denial is a pretense. The uncertainty of loss and the pain of the void it leaves can be overwhelming. This makes it easy to avoid, cover up, or pretend that the loss either doesn't exist or doesn't adversely impact you. When you do not embrace the reality of what has happened to you, it will only leave you with a false sense of recovery, and a delay in the true healing process.

Suppressed pain and emotions will eventually seep out into all kinds of mental and behavioral disorders or physical sicknesses. Displaying outward signs of forging forward by attempting to prove you are as good or competent as you were before the loss, does not mean you have embraced the reality of loss.

> Failure to embrace the reality of what happened leads to a false sense of recovery and delays the true healing process.

Examine yourself very closely to be sure it isn't pretense. I've learned that to do a self-examination effectively, it takes the person who knows you the best to assist in this process—the one who will be absolutely honest and truthful, yet without criticism or condemnation. Yeah, it's going to take no one less than God Himself for this task. Now, this doesn't mean He can't use people who are spiritually and ethically mature who are close to you. But, the idea is that to get a *clear* picture, you will need help. If not, you will end up with your subjective view of yourself, and could potentially do more harm than good.

Another common escape from the reality of loss is to become absorbed and consumed with what I call the logistics of the loss—why it happened, why it shouldn't have happened, who is to blame, is this fair or unfair, or any related thinking that will keep you stuck and unable to get the help you need. The answer to all or some of these things may be crucial to your recovery process, but during the initial stage of crisis, it is very dangerous for this line of thinking to dominate. It only becomes a distraction and will make it very difficult for you to sooner rather than later embrace the reality that what happened did happen.

Your heart and possibly your body has taken a very devastating blow; your reasoning faculties have been thrown into shambles and are full-blown faulty. If you've just been hit by a missile that cost you something you love dearly, that's not the time to try to figure it all out. Think about it this way; when a soldier is on the front line of war, and they are hit in the chest by a bullet, neither he nor his comrades are going to stand by wondering, "How did this happen?" "Who was supposed to cover for me?" Or "What kind of missile struck me?" No! The soldier will try to get to a place of safety. His comrades will rally around him, tell him to keep still, don't talk, and try to relax until they can get him stabilized. It is a very critical time for the soldier. There are no demands or expectations put on him except to hold on and try to stay conscious.

Experiencing life-altering crisis is no different. When we are hit by a missile of personal loss, it is a process to get you stabilized, assess the damage, attend to the damage, and then recover. Whatever condition the situation left you in is what your life is until you garner the strength to bring to bear another reality. You have what you have, you feel what you feel, and it is what it is. Does it mean your life is over? No. Does it mean you will always feel the way it has left you feeling? No. Does it mean there will be difficult days ahead? Yes. Does it mean it will take some effort and determination on your part? Yes. However, no matter how unbearable and painful it may be, hope is available. As long as you keep breathing, you are a possible candidate for healing and recovery.

Embracing the reality does not mean getting stuck or succumbing to the circumstances. The way you will face and manage in the crisis of loss, will be determined by how you have lived and managed your life before the loss. The loss you may have encountered has changed your life as you knew it, and now you will have to change. Personal loss brings change, and it demands change, but your life does not have to end with the change.

Let me share with you three reasons why so many people get stuck and cannot seem to find the courage or strength to move forward.

Lost Their Individuality

What I mean by this is that they have convinced themselves that the thing or the person they have lost made or validated them. Now that whatever was lost is gone, they don't know who they are or why they are. In essence, they allowed the person or thing to define them, so now without it, they are stuck. The truth is, no thing or person can ever properly define another person. When it is allowed, it will never end well.

"Self"ishness

This will keep anyone stuck. This is especially true when it is the loss of a person either from ending a relationship or death. In some cases, the pain is not so much the loss of the person, as it is how the loss has left you; the one left behind is disadvantaged. If a person has left you in a relationship, they are gone because that is what they wanted for them. Whether you were rightly or wrongly treated, a relationship takes two people wanting and trying to make it work. If they are gone, don't try to hold them or manipulate them to stay because you will do yourself an injustice. Don't stay stuck and be depressed because you can't make someone want to be with you.

Likewise, as foreign as physical death will always be to us, true love and an unselfish person would never want to hold on to a loved one who has lived a life of physical suffering and pain day after day, or left to deteriorate in a vegetable state. Holding someone in those states is not for them, it is for you. Unfortunately, I know of people who have prayed to God to raise their loved ones up—not for the one's sake who was plagued but because they wanted them here for themselves. I have even seen individuals become very angry at the deceased for leaving them and would stay angry for years about it. It would be so much more beneficial and considerate to let the person go to rest than to suffer. The one left behind should not inflict suffering on themselves holding unforgiveness or anger for being left. That is indeed being stuck in a victim mentality, and very selfish. In the end, selfishness will always keep you stuck on you.

Guilt

Guilt is probably the most common. When dealing with loss, feelings of guilt usually stem from the individual seeing themselves as having failed in meeting the expectations or responsibility of what they have lost. Whether that is true or not, they are plagued with the idea of not measuring up. Somehow they convince themselves that they are to be blamed or contributed to the blame. It is hard to believe that ego would be found at a most vulnerable time as personal loss, but in some cases it is. Somehow, the guilt feelings are often masked under, "How am I going to be perceived?" "What will people think of me?" "I'm ashamed of what I did or didn't do." They carry around a "woe is me" "it's my fault" mindset, while the ego gets a twisted sense of ease and justification for whatever you actually did or did not do before the loss happened. Either way, there is nothing redemptive in allowing thoughts of guilt and regret to hold you in bondage. You make a choice to let it go and endeavor to move forward with your life in a way in which there will be no cause for guilt again.

If you are in fact guilty, there is a way to relieve yourself of the guilt. If the offense involves others that are yet living, you can always ask them to pardon (forgive) you for their hurt or inconvenience even if it is yourself you need to forgive. If the persons are not accessible to you or not living, the act of forgiveness will have to come from you forgiving yourself. Holding yourself in the bondage of unforgiveness is not going to make right what you have done wrong. Repentance (acknowledging and turning from your wrong) and forgiveness are the only things that can release you from the guilt of offense.

We will now take a look at the next step:

"For to be carnally minded is death, but to be spiritually minded is life and peace." (Romans 8:6)

STEP 3

ALLOW THE RECOVERY PROCESS

WHEN LIFE BROADSIDES you, your approach cannot be business as usual. There are some life-altering encounters that demand a complete halt and full engagement. I have the perfect example. I was always the person whose philosophy of life's challenges was that you take the hit, get up, and move on. However, when I found myself face to face with divorce, I was forced to disengage from what I knew as normal and fully engage in the foreign world of divorce and recovery. The grief process was absolutely necessary, and because everything in our lives is so well connected, in times like this the known and the unknown, the good and the not so good will surface.

In some loss, the ability to move forward may first require an intervention outside of yourself. There may be some things that you experience during the grief process that are completely foreign and could leave you overwhelmed with feelings that appear to be beyond your natural capacity to handle. The nature of the loss and how it impacted you will determine how long your specific recovery process will take. You must not try to rush too quickly to move forward with making major decisions or allow people or circumstances to dictate your progress.

We all process differently. It's important that you allow yourself the space and time to recover. The grief process should be used to help you recover, not to overtake you and keep you stuck. While the circumstances may be out of your control, your focus is to maintain control of yourself, and more specifically, your thoughts and emotions. In the midst of the pain, you can decide that your loss is not the end. As difficult as grieving is, it is of utmost importance for all those emotions to surface. They must be identified so that they are not suppressed and sabotage you in the future.

Here are some important things to remember during the grief and recovery process.

It Begins on the Inside

The process of recovering from loss must begin on the inside of you. It's important to realize that this loss is not the end of your life. The emotions you feel are not permanent unless you decide to make them permanent. You will not always feel the way you may feel today. Give yourself permission to grieve. Keep your mind and heart open to change even if you don't fully understand what it all means at the moment. Likewise, you must give yourself permission to let go of grieving when it is time. Ending the grieving process does not mean you will no longer feel the pain or disappointment. In spite of what you may be feeling, you will decide that you cannot maintain the old way of thinking or the same posture or attitude in how you approach your life. Everything does not have to be figured out all at once, so keep in mind that it is a process.

> While the circumstances may be out of your control, maintain control of yourself, your thoughts and your emotions.

Time and Patience

Be aware that the process takes time and requires patience. A part of the grief and recovery process is rebuilding and redefining. If your loss has left you with the core of your life (foundation) shattered, the process may take longer than what you feel you are willing or able to manage. Impatience will keep your desire for recovery farther and farther away.

Rushing into counterfeit, premature, and temporary solutions for the sake of gaining comfort is like putting a band-aid on a gunshot wound. The damage is too deep and too wide for a band-aid. You don't want to make the mistake of covering the hole in your soul up with something or someone who does not have the capacity to make you whole.

The reality is that there will be other losses as long as we are alive on the planet. The goal is that we allow the complete process to take place so that our lives are put back together with things of substance, things that will add strength, courage, and hope.

Pride Hinders

The subtlety of pride is a great hindrance to your process. It's quite interesting that during a time when love and support are needed the most, pride would be the primary culprit to show up to influence us. Pride is like an invisible person who whispers in your ear at the most vulnerable time of struggle. This is particularly true when people are extending themselves to you to empathize or express acts of kindness. You may find yourself thinking like this: "I don't want anyone feeling sorry for me. I can do this myself. I don't want people to think that I'm weak or vulnerable." If that kind of thinking is not addressed and corrected, you will consciously or subconsciously begin to drive people away from you, some of which may be instrumental in your full recovery.

People who are challenged with pride in times of crisis or loss are usually those who are accustomed to always being or wanting to be in control. The loss has proven to them that they are not in control. Therefore, the idea of them having to be subjected or dependent, in a different way, is very frightening to them. Pride is a hindrance to the process because it does not allow you to trust, or surrender to the much-needed help that is many times right before you.

> *"Being confident of this very thing, that He who has begun a good work in you will complete it until the day of Jesus Christ."* (Philippians 1:6)

STEP 4

LET GO

SOMETIMES WHAT IS lost may be physically removed from your life, but that does not mean you have let it go. If it is gone and over, it's now a part of your past. Attempting to hold on to two realities – what was and what is – at the same time keeps you stuck between the two, and prevents you from moving forward because you are stuck. You will have to let go of one to embrace the other fully.

Imagine going on a vacation having an amazing experience. After bathing in pleasure for seven wonderful days, it's time to return to what we call reality. You have to leave the five-star resort where you have been pampered. The ocean is no longer your front yard. The exotic foods and drinks are a thing of the past because you got to go to work! Monday morning at work, the boss is demanding those reports by noon, coffee from the machine in the office is a far cry from the flavored cappuccinos by the pool you had a few days ago. You're having flashbacks. Just as you are recapping the day before you left, you took a dive off this beautiful waterfall, you then hear a phone ring and snap back realizing it was only a mini vision of last week.

While you were in that mental state of drifting back into vacation, you momentarily let go of where you were in your thoughts or even your actions; you left work. The phone ringing now brings you back to reality, and it is the boss calling you with budget questions. You hear yourself rambling and stumbling over your words trying to give answers you don't have. At the end of the day, you look at your clock and realize that this struggle of trying to hold two realities has cost you a whole day and nothing productive has gotten done as this day ends. You are stuck!

The vacation is over and is now a part of your past. However, as long as you attempt to keep it alive in your now you will struggle with being distracted, frustrated, and unproductive at work. This example is not to make light of your loss and I am not suggesting that you shouldn't have thoughts and memories. Rather I want to give you a word picture of how you will find yourself in a rut that gets deeper and deeper if you hold on to what was. What's worse is when this struggle is associated with negative things. For example, when reminiscing brings about negative feelings like depression, sadness, regret, and the like.

During my recovery process, I once struggled with letting go of some things that seemed to play in my head like a broken record. It was almost tormenting. The thoughts just seemed to have a mind of their own. One day, I was having a conversation about it with a friend, and they told me rather than giving over to the thoughts or trying to push them out of my head, I should take control by giving myself permission. I didn't understand what that meant so I asked for the simple version.

> Give yourself permission to think about the situation only for a designated time each day for a set number of minutes.

They said that I should give myself permission to think about the situation only for a designated time each day allowing myself a set number of minutes. Just hearing that idea gave me such a sense of empowerment and taking charge, so I did it. No matter what the thoughts were, I only gave myself permission for the designated number of minutes. This seemed so simple but yet it was so powerful! As I began to do that exercise, I then took my control a step further. I began to decide what those thoughts would be, and how many of my overall minutes I would give to each train of thought. Every time I took steps toward managing my thoughts, it was easier and easier for me to begin to control my life in that present time.

I learned that it was detrimental to my recovery to live in past memories or live out of those memories. Life has to be lived now not in or from our past. Whether you have mastered letting go or not, at least you must acknowledge that you need to and that you are willing to. I know it is hard and I'm very sorry if you are yet struggling, but you have to do this in order to move forward. You can do it. There's also another great danger in holding on to what is finished. Your heart gets confused, and it begins to try to duplicate what you hold before it through your thoughts or conversations. Although your mind understands that what you are giving your attention to has passed, your heart doesn't. Your heart just goes on automatic and tries to reproduce. I believe out of this comes what we know as obsessive compulsive behavior. What a vicious cycle! It keeps you in a loop and quest that is never fulfilled.

> *"Brethren, I do not count myself to have apprehended; but one thing I do, forgetting those things which are behind and reaching forward to those things which are ahead."* (Philippians 3:13)

STEP 5

CREATE NEW NORMALS

AFTER ALLOWING STEPS one and two to become a springboard for the next phase of your process, you will find that you are better prepared to confront the things of your life that your loss would have answered. You must now take the time to determine how to reassess and respond to this new way of life.

It's when you fully accept and embrace that your old normal doesn't exist anymore that the true recovery process begins. The new normal or normals will then unfold as you move forward. For many, creating a new normal is very challenging, but if you follow through, it can be the most refreshing part of the process. If you are not a self-starter, you will have to push harder to get going.

In order for anything to change, there has to be movement. Movement is always an indicator that there is life in something. In a sense, you are now ready to begin to give life to what's left of your life! You have to do something. I have a very practical and simple recommendations for you to begin this part of the process:

- Take a pen and paper and list at least <u>five</u> things you were able to do before the loss occurred that you are unable to, or have difficulty doing now.

- On opposite side of the paper come up with <u>five</u> other things you can do instead of the five losses you listed. Take your time and stretch your creative mind. You can do this. These should be things you will get some enjoyment out of. They could even be things you have thought about but never had the opportunity to do until now. Don't be afraid to dream! Although you may not get the same pleasure, or benefit as before, at least make the list interesting things that will add to your life. It may well be something you have never considered. As long as it is something responsible and it is realistic, it's good.

- The idea here is that the pain of the loss is not to completely fill your emotional space so that you will not become a victim to what doesn't exist anymore. Think about the list of five things for a few days, then try to list at least <u>one</u> thing you can do now as a starting point to move toward it. Make a decision that no matter how difficult it is, you will apply the first step of the new normal you have listed.

- Right next to each first step you will commit to assigning a date when you will get this accomplished. (Remember you're taking charge of your life.)

One more thought on this, it is virtually impossible to create new normals without breaking bad habits and replacing them with new ones. There is a proven method for creating new habits, which I learned from a mentor of mine years ago. It goes like this: Whatever you do *repetitiously* will eventually become *easy*. Human nature has proven that it is in those things that are easy where we find the most *pleasure*. Finally, when something becomes pleasurable, we inevitably will do it more *often*.

> It is virtually impossible to create new normals without breaking bad habits and replacing them with great habits.

Then ultimately, habits are broken and created by doing the same thing consistently. Now, I'm sure you will agree that the most difficult part of this process is starting. Your desire to make life work again–or maybe even better than before in spite of the devastation of a great loss–has to overrule the temptation to sit in the mud and quit with a victim mentality.

On a separate sheet of paper with a line drawn down the middle do this:

- On one side write down at least <u>seven</u> unpleasant and unfruitful thought habits or action habits you may have developed since you experienced the loss.

- On the other side of the paper write down at least <u>one</u> thing opposite of the unpleasant and unfruitful habit which you can begin to apply the REPOH method. The acronym is as follows: **R**epetition-**E**asy-**P**leasure-**O**ften-**H**abit

- For example, let's say that your life-altering crisis of loss left you struggling to get things done. You find yourself having lost interest in most things and procrastinating about almost everything. Your REPOH affirmation would go like this.

> *As I repetitiously stop procrastinating to get things done, getting things done becomes easy. When getting things done becomes easy, getting things done becomes*

pleasurable, when getting things done becomes pleasurable, getting things done will occur with me more often, when getting things done occurs more often, getting things done becomes a habit!

"But be doers of the word, and not hearers only, deceiving yourselves." (James 1:22)

STEP 6

ASSESS YOURSELF

ASSESSING OURSELVES AND thinking about the kind of person we are or giving long consideration as to why we are the way we are is not something the average person gives much time to. I know how it is when you've been hit so hard with life that you don't want to be held accountable for anyone or anything. You want to be left alone to nurse your pain and disappointment. What I learned is that those are the times when you are wide open to vulnerability, and being open can help you learn some pretty interesting things about yourself. There is also something about crisis that demands who we are, what we believe, and how we are, to come to the forefront. It's very easy to avoid the mirror of our own heart, particularly if all we see in that mirror is hurt. It can be very painful in and of itself.

In many cases, if you are open to assessing ourselves, you will find that the loss that you think is causing you so much pain and discomfort, may not be the real core or the root of why your feelings are so out of control. Sometimes the loss just gives a valid justification for a much deeper problem within, to surface out of control emoting.

On the other hand, anything that you are involved in for any length of time will shape your thinking and ultimately your behavior. Looking at your *self* means that you are willing and able to separate anything or anyone from the crisis and see only *you*. After spending 27 years giving all I had to give in a marriage, rearing two children, and making sacrifices I didn't even know I was capable of, I found myself faced with divorce. The person I had become in those 27 years was not the same woman I was before the marriage and children. While being absorbed in the marriage and the family relationship during those 27 years, I didn't see the need to *consider* much of who I was, but rather I just *lived* who I was. Once the loss occurred, it was necessary for me to assess not only the fall-out from the loss in the light of who I had become, but I had to assess myself.

This may be the hardest part of the process for some because, like me, you may not be accustomed to paying attention to yourself. But for me, I wanted to do whatever was necessary to get whole and never have to visit that kind of devastation again. During the assessment, you may find that you developed a misplaced dependence on what you lost, without having any healthy boundaries set. In this case, it can be difficult to separate the thing or the person you *lost* from who you *are*.

In cases like this, you'll soon see that you have become very needy and unsure of your ability to stand on your own. On a positive note, you may equally find that you have developed characteristics that are strong and healthy, that will help in the process of starting over. Either way, the good of who you have become or the bad of it, you must do an assessment to get in touch with yourself.

> Take the good and the strength of who you have become and use those character traits to build upon for your new reality.

The worst thing is trying to move on without this part of the process only to find yourself having to repeat the same or similar loss. The idea is that you take the good and the strength of who you have become and use those character traits to build upon for your new reality. The not so good, or weaknesses you will find about yourself must be left behind to avoid keeping you stuck. Most times, outside help is needed in this area.

Please let me encourage you, whatever you do, do not try to prematurely add someone else in the equation of a process that has to be realized by you alone. It is not fair or convenient for you or the other person. If you are broken and hurting, all you can give to someone is broken and hurting. Get healthy first!

> *"Examine yourselves as to whether you are in the faith. Test yourselves. Do you not know yourselves, that Jesus Christ is in you?"* (2 Corinthians 13:5a)

STEP 7

START OVER

THERE IS AN old saying, "Nothing beats a failure but a try." This ideology is quite appropriate here. The prefix *re* means that you are doing something that has been done before. This is the starting over point, and it requires you to do something. The loss, no matter what it was, is no longer a part of your life's equation. Although it may have felt like it, your life did not end with the loss. It (your life) is waiting for you to start it over again!

Today, you may more than likely still be experiencing pain, disappointment, shame, sadness, and the sorts, from your loss. However, for a window of time you will give attention to the fact that starting right out of those emotional deficits, you can grasp the hope of an opportunity to expand, create, or build something of yourself that you have not known before. The same energy and expectation you start the starting over process with will determine the results you achieve. The biggest question asked at this juncture is, "Where do I start?" My answer is what I call "The 3PS."

Prioritize

Your loss may have left so many areas in your life unsettled and vulnerable, which means it may be hard to determine where the starting over point begins with you. Trying to address everything at the same time will only lead to confusion and feelings of being overwhelmed, which will inevitably leave you doing nothing. Take the time to determine the top three things that need your immediate attention. Do not hesitate to ask for the help of someone who is close and trustworthy to help you with this as well. Sometimes it is good to have someone who is outside of your personal life to bring a different perspective on the matters. Just remember, all of your emotions are in high gear right now. It will be so easy to make decisions out of those emotions. However, someone neutral to challenge or question why you would make one thing a priority over another may be the best thing for you. Once you have listed the most crucial three and you feel like you have somewhat of a handle on them, your sense of gaining control of your life will propel you and give you the courage to move to another three.

Plan

Your plan basically says what and how you will move toward the priorities you set. Writing it out will also help hold you accountable to yourself. The plan will also serve as a guide for you to follow your progress. It is very important that you are able to see and measure your progress so that you maintain your focus and courage to move forward. If at any time the circumstances change, the plan may need to change also. While it is okay to be flexible, it is still very important that you know where you are going and your plan to get there. A key aspect of developing your plan is that your approach to answering your priorities is realistic and not premature. If you have lost a job that you started working right out of college, and 20 years later you are laid off, you would not use the same type of resume you did 20 years ago. Before applying you may want to research or re-educate yourself in the field; you will find that a lot has changed in 20 years. Your plan may change with the idea of considering a different field altogether. For me, after working in a non-profit organization for over 20 years, it was necessary

> Your life did not end with the loss. Your life is waiting for you to start it over again!

for me to go into an entirely different field when I found myself trying to re-enter the workforce. I had absolutely no background in finance, but a position I once held almost 20 years ago was now housed under the Finance Department, so I had to make the necessary adjustments. It is what opened up for me, and I had to step into the position bravely. Don't be afraid to stay flexible. On the other hand, maybe you lost a long-term relationship that left you hurt and confused because you didn't see it coming. Now three months later you are planning to enter another one. You may want to pace yourself and give yourself time to recover before opening yourself up in your already vulnerable state. The plan must be sensible, and not something that could potentially cause a repeat of the last loss.

Practice

Once your plan is solvent, it is time to practice what you want. Taking a leap of faith by putting things into motion can be liberating and scary at the same time. Whatever your loss has caused you to do or not to do, the practice is the time you begin to do it or not do it again—starting over! One of the biggest obstacles here is the fear of failure. Fear is very real and can be tormenting, but it's only strength is what you give it. The reality is that as you begin to live again, take charge of your life, and move forward to re-establish your life, the most well-thought-out plan is going to have bumps in the road. But remember, practice means you keep doing it and keep doing it until you get it right. You will find that your life without what you lost, will eventually begin to unfold into the new. If it is things you have lost, things can be replaced. If it is parts of yourself you have lost, because you are still breathing, restoration and recovery are available. If it is people you have lost in relationships, you can cultivate new relationships if you don't shut down. If you have lost loved ones in death, there can never be a replacement of those individuals personally, but if you desire a same type of relationship, the world is full of people who want the same. Finally, if you decide your new life is better without replacing, restoring or reconciling what was lost, let your decision be without the influence of fear, and practice your new life.

> *"Now to Him who is able to do exceedingly abundantly above all that we ask or think, according to the power that works in us, to Him be glory in the church by Christ Jesus to all generations, forever and ever. Amen."* (Ephesians 3:20-21)

STEP 8

EMBRACE YOUR NEW

THIS IS THE ultimate goal—embracing your new! Here is where you find life is a blank canvas. Don't be afraid to tread into the unfamiliar. This crisis may have taken a lot from you, but some good things have been left in you also. Contrary to what you may be able to imagine right now, *all* is not lost! I remember when I had to take ownership of my life–empty and undesirable as it was. After a few years of unsuccessfully trying to bring someone else into my brokenness, I pretty much had to force myself to see it was just not going to work. The healing and restoration of my soul and redefining of my life was not designed for company. no, it was something I had to walk through on my own. It felt like my life had bottomed out and everything I knew as a way of life was lost. I was divorced after 27 years, diagnosed and survived cancer, laid off from my employment after 23 years and a 55 year old with no place of my own to live. The odds of me starting life over in the face of all this were very high naturally. Nevertheless, with my faith in God and a determination to live, I found the courage to embrace my new life.

As shattered and disconnected as the circumstances had left me, I was alive, and I had to give myself permission to keep on living. Embrace your life as it is and trust God to show you how to take baby steps to build it from here. The thing about being stuck in life is that the longer you stay in that state, the harder it is for you to find the courage to get out! Many times, the biggest battle is with ourselves. I remember a point in my process of recovery from divorce at which I made a resolve that I would never get used to being single again. I absolutely hated being single, especially after being married for so long. Not knowing what to do with myself, I would shy away from doing anything new alone. It just felt like I was somehow settling into not being in a relationship or not being married. I had no idea I was digging myself deeper and deeper into an isolated hole.

I remember one of the first times I got dressed up, made reservations and took myself to dinner. How could something so simple be so intimidating? Well, I did it anyway, and by the time I got to the restaurant, my stomach was in a nervous knot. First of all, it looked like it was couple's night! It looked like everyone there was with someone, and they all were watching me! For every excuse I tried to come up with before I took that leap of faith, I lived it out right there in that moment. Quite frankly, the struggle was in my mind, but even if what I felt was indeed happening why had I allowed it to affect me? These are the kind of questions I began to ask myself. I wanted to get to the real core of why being alone was such a frightening and awkward thing for me.

As I continued to stretch outside of my self-made boundaries, I learned so much about myself. I got to see the person that 27 years of marriage had made me become. I found some things in me that I had buried and needed to be brought back to life; and there were some things I knew if I didn't change my way of thinking, I would never realize the benefits of embracing life again.

The first steps of embracing your new life will have to begin inside of you. As I did, you may have to give yourself permission to live, to take risk, to push yourself to move forward in this new season of your life.

The definition of *embrace* according to Merriam-Webster Dictionary is "to take up especially readily or gladly." The loss may have taken away something or someone that you cannot physically get back.

However, if as a result your courage was taken, your ability to trust, your strength, your faith, or even your desire, take it up again! There is more to be had! This is your life, and only you can create and embrace what the rest of it will look like.

Right now, you may be thinking, "It's easier said than done." And, you are absolutely right; most times it is. But do you know that you don't have to do it on your own? I could never have gotten through on my own. The truth is, God never intended for us to try to manage life on our own, the good or the bad of it. If you ask Him to help you, He will help you.

> *"God is our refuge and strength, A very present help in trouble."* (Psalms 46:1)

Some people will never ask God to help them because they are angry with Him. They have judged Him guilty because they believe that whatever happened to cause all of their pain and suffering was ultimately caused by Him. Not very many people will verbally admit that they feel that way, but it is the underlining thought in their conscious and subconscious mind. Another truth is that God is not psychotic or sadistic. He did not send His Son into the world to save us from sin and corruption, to then turn around and practice sin and corruption on us. The Bible is very clear about who our problem is in Jesus' own words.

"I am the door. If anyone enters by Me, he will be saved, and will go in and out and find pasture. The thief does not come except to steal, and to kill, and to destroy. I have come that they may have life, and that they may have it more abundantly." (John 10:9-10)

There is so much life ahead of you to be lived. I pray that God will shine in your heart to give revelation of how awesome it is that you are here, with this amazing opportunity to see life and do life in ways that perhaps you have yet experienced. Take your life back, present it to Him, and enjoy the rest of your journey!

ABOUT THE AUTHOR

BRENDA DANIEL IS an inspirational writer, motivational speaker, and ordained minister. She is the founder of Global WIIND, a para-church organization that offers consulting services, personal development coaching, and leadership/mobilization training. These services are offered to churches, interest groups, individuals and private companies. As a Kingdom Ambassador, Brenda has trained and organized teams for short and long-term missions work to 24 countries.

Often referred to as Coach, the essence of her calling is to train and teach, with the sole intent to help people reach their full potential and purpose for life. This passion is a constant expression in her messages and writing style.

In her own experience with loss and recovery, she has faced three major life-altering crises all occurring just months apart: divorce from a 27-year marriage, terminal illness, and loss of employment. Brenda knows well the struggles and temptations of loss. Brenda's testimony about how she recovered is, "It all was way beyond my own capacity. It took me marrying the spiritual to the practical to gain my life back!"

AUTHOR CONTACT

Brenda Daniel
P. O. Box 424
Inglewood, CA 90306
Globalwiindmtc@gmail.com
www.GlobalWIIND.org
Facebook.com/globalwiind